MW00966868

# My Secret Hideaway

## Communion With God

by

Larry W. Colwell

authorHOUSE™

1663 LIBERTY DRIVE, SUITE 200
BLOOMINGTON, INDIANA 47403
(800) 839-8640
WWW.AUTHORHOUSE.COM

First published by AuthorHouse 12/01/05

ISBN: 1-4259-0755-5 (e)
ISBN: 1-4208-9211-8 (sc)

Library of Congress Control Number: 2005909160

Printed in the United States of America
Bloomington, Indiana

This book is printed on acid-free paper.

## DEDICATION

*This book is dedicated to the memory of my now deceased father-in-law, Rev. P. James Preston, Sr., who often used the prophetic phrase, "Don't move, improve." Also, to my mom, Mrs. Lenora C. Wiggins, who has been supportive, loving and caring during the preparation of this book and throughout my life.*

# *ACKNOWLEDGEMENTS*

*I would like to thank and acknowledge the following people who encouraged me and believed that I could accomplish this task in the creation of this book. First, my wife, Neldra, for her unyielding support in anything and everything I attempt to do; second, my daughter, Annel, for contributing several poems and diligently providing scriptural references to a number of poems in the book; third, my mom, sister, (Margaret) and son, (Dennis), for taking the time to listen to and make candid comments and suggestions on some of the poems; Finally, a number of members in my church family who never ceased to ask about the progress of the book. Thank you all so much. You have truly been an inspiration and blessing!*

*Larry W. Colwell*

# INTRODUCTION

*As with my first book, "I'll See You Tomorrow," writing continues to be a focal point in my life. Poetry, which conveys feelings and emotions, tends to reach a person's heart and soul. Many artists today use poetry for such expressions. Poetry is my chosen way of expressing my ideas. As I write, I try to incorporate these same expressions in my poems. When you read my poems written here, you will note several rhyme schemes. Though poetry does not have to rhyme, I find that it is a way of capturing the reader's attention. Most of my poems are "inspirational" with a message that, hopefully, will appeal to the reader who desires a closer walk with God. Other poems in the book are on the lighter side and will evoke laughter, sadness etc. I hope that you will enjoy this second book of poetry.*

# TRIBUTE

It is my pleasure, as a son, to commend the work of my father for your enjoyment and encouragement. Not all sons would consider such an act to be a pleasure. Perhaps in some perfunctory manner other sons might be moved to write words of honor for their fathers. However, this is not the case for me, as my own true love for my father is my impetus.

My father has put a lot of time and effort into this collection of poetry. However, it is not the time and effort alone that should cause one to read the pieces. No, it is the product of the time and effort: the content of the pieces themselves. When I was given the opportunity to read early versions of many of the works within the collection, I was deeply challenged and humbled. I say this especially with regard to the inspirational/Christian works. These specific works caused me to look at my own personal relationship with Christ Jesus and assess the depth and breadth of that relationship. I came away feeling a greater thirsting and hunger for more of God's presence and preeminence in my life. I tend to think that any work that can, in the positive sense, stir your heart to move closer to God in spirit and truth must have a mark of His presence upon it. To that end, I commend this collection to anyone desiring "just a closer walk with thee." While not all the pieces focus on the spiritual, all pieces come from the heart of a man who has experienced and continues to experience a spiritual renewal in his soul. For all readers, including myself, I hope these works, as expressed through my father's heart and hands, will lead us all to our own "secret hideaways" for daily renewal. If it is the case that you don't have a "hideaway" for yourself, I think there is enough content within the book to help you find your way there.

Dad, I love you. You are forever my hero and inspiration. As I've said before, if I can grow and live to be half the man you are, I will consider my life well spent and successful. Continue to pursue Christ, laying hold to Him even as He holds you.

8 September 2005

-Son, Dennis

# DEDICATION

*"I always thank God for you because of His grace given you in Christ Jesus. For in Him you have been enriched in every way—in all your speaking and in all your knowledge."*

*1 Corinthians 1:4-5 (NIV)*

*God did it again! He stirred up your gift of writing poetry into book number two. As you communed with God in the secret recesses of your heart and soul, God guided your thoughts to write more and more about His beloved Son, Jesus Christ. Every day has been a day of Thanksgiving to see how Gods has worked through you as He flooded your heart with sometimes two and three poems at a time. It's been truly amazing to see God at work in you.*

*I thank God for gifting you with the ability to communicate through the written word. I thank you for being obedient to write down what God would have you communicate to the world about His Son, Jesus.*

*May you continue to glorify God in all that you do and say. God bless you, my beloved husband.*

*Love always,*
*Neldra*

# TABLE OF CONTENTS

DEDICATION ................................................................v

ACKNOWLEDGEMENTS ...............................................vii

INTRODUCTION.........................................................ix

TRIBUTE ..................................................................xi

DEDICATION ...........................................................xiii

## INSPIRATION

MY WISH....................................................................3

I'LL DO THE BEST I CAN – Rev. P. James Preston, Sr..................5

MY SECRET HIDEAWAY ..............................................7

SERENITY .................................................................9

THE SHIP (OF SALVATION) .......................................11

THE CANDLE ON THE CORNER..................................13

MATCHING SHOES (Walking Through Time) ................15

THE WASHING MACHINE ........................................17

THE WIND ..............................................................19

THE LIGHTHOUSE ..................................................21

THE WHEELBARROW ..............................................23

CHAINS .................................................................25

FLIGHT ..................................................................27

HIJACKED ..............................................................29

A.I.D.S. Advising Individuals Devoted to Satan ............31

C.I.A. (Christ In Action).............................................33

D.O.C. 'J' (Depending On Christ) Jesus .......................35

MESSAGE IN A BOTTLE ...........................................37

CLEAN UP YOUR ACT (Jesus is Coming) ....................39

THE PASSION ..........................................................41

THE REMORSEFUL THIEF ........................................43

THE PARTY ................................................45

THE SHEPHERD IN THE STICKS..............................47

CHURCH FOLK: PASS THE PLATE! ...........................49

CHURCH FOLK: CHURCH MEETING............................51

THE CHRISTIAN SOLDIER ..................................53

SIGNS ..................................................55

MY PRAYER...............................................57

LITTLE THINGS ..........................................59

LABOR OF LOVE ..........................................61

IN THE COUNTRY .........................................63

I'LL BE SATISFIED.......................................65

IT NEVER CROSSED MY MIND ...............................67

CHALLENGES .............................................69

BEYOND THE OPEN SEA ....................................71

FAMILY/RELATIONS

BEFORE THE FLOOD .......................................75

THESE TIMES.............................................77

THE PROMISE ............................................79

THE JAR.................................................81

A MISSING SON ..........................................83

FATHER TO SON ..........................................85

BE A MAN................................................87

THE ENCOUNTER ..........................................89

FIRST DATE .............................................91

INTERVENTION............................................93

THE JADED MASK..........................................95

MORNING MATTERS.........................................97

## MAKING A DIFFERENCE

THE VERSATILE LADY ................................................ 101

MR. IGGADEE .......................................................... 103

THE BALLAD OF THE DUMMY - PT 1 ................................ 105

THE BALLAD OF THE DUMMY – PT 2 .............................. 107

THE EMPATHETIC DUMMY ......................................... 109

## BIBLE HEROES & HEROINES

ORDINARY FOLK ..................................................... 113

THE STORM ........................................................... 115

THE ROADSIDE SHACK ............................................. 117

THE ROD ............................................................... 119

HAGAR - by Annel C. Cooke ....................................... 123

RUTH'S RAP - by Annel C. Cooke ................................. 125

## TRIBUTES

GOD'S CHOSEN FLOWER (In memory of Claudia Y. Bullock) 129

TRIBUTE TO REV. AND SIS. AUSTIN – S.T.A.R.S. ............... 131

TRIBUTE TO PASTOR & SIS. AUSTIN– MAY 2004 ............. 133

EBC'S CARPENTERS ................................................ 135

# Inspiration

# MY WISH

My wish for you is happiness
All through the coming year
And hope you take advantage of
The words I've written here.

You've proven that your faith in God
Has prepared a way for you
To open up your heart to Him
And show your love so true.

He told us we should prepare ourselves
For we know not the hour or day
When He will pass this way, once more,
And carry us away.

Rejoice my brothers, sisters and saints
The Lord is coming again
To keep a promise He made to us,
When we were deep in sin.

# I'LL DO THE BEST I CAN
## – Rev. P. James Preston, Sr.

(Dedicated to Miss A. M. Anglin, 2-18-
43[who later became his wife])

Trials of life are sure to come,
     I may not understand;
But God will make a way for me,
     So I'll do the best I can.

I've never dreamed of giving up!
     I have in mind a plan;
If I fail to reach the top,
     I'll do the best I can.

No matter what fate holds for me,
     On ocean, sea or land;
I know I shall reap my just reward,
     I'll do the best I can.

I'll always make sure I am right,
     There-by take a stand;
I am giving the world the best I have,
     I'll do the best I can.

# MY SECRET HIDEAWAY

There is a place I love to go,
My thoughts and I alone,
Away from worldly pleasures,
Into my comfort zone.
It's not too far from anywhere;
I make it in a day.
I pack my bags and travel
To my secret hideaway.

While I am there, my time is spent
Involved in spiritual food,
Filling up with scriptures
Amidst my solitude.
There's nothing there to steal my soul
Or tamper with my mind,
Or break my concentration
Or take my precious time.

I'm hungry and I'm thirsty
For the knowledge of His word.
I'm anxious and excited
When He calls on me to serve.
I open up my Bible,
Then I stop to kneel and pray.
I commune with God and nature
In my secret hideaway.

The spirit has enraptured me,
I truly do believe,
When everything is finished there
I pack my bags to leave.
And when I think about the time,
It was a pleasant stay
Communing with the Master
In my secret hideaway.

DEVOTIONAL THOUGHT:

*"Now in the morning, having risen a long while before daylight, He went out and departed to a solitary place, and there He prayed."* Mark 1:35 NKJV

# SERENITY

I rise up early to start my day
And prepare myself to leave,
To journey to my favorite spot
Where the blessings I'll receive.

The way is calm, the path is straight
As I make my way without,
And think about the things I'll do,
As I travel my usual route.

I don't take much to eat or drink,
For I'll be in a pensive mood,
And gladly answer my Father's calling
With a fervent attitude.

The dock is where I'll take my seat
And gaze upon the waters.
I'll quietly wait here at this place
To receive my spiritual orders.

Lord, what's your plan for me today?
What will you have me do?
I've come to offer up my time
As I wait patiently on you.

When my Father speaks at last,
I come to realize
That I must try to fill this day
With what my Lord supplies.

So, I journey back the way I came,
My mind and I at rest.
I've received my spiritual food today,
And, once again, I'm blessed!

DEVOTIONAL THOUGHT:
*"Now in the morning, having risen a long while before daylight, He went out and departed to a solitary place, and there He prayed."* Mark 1:35  NKJV

# THE SHIP (OF SALVATION)

A ship is traveling swiftly
Over the rough and rolling sea.
There's something unique about it
As it transfigures you and me.

It's an ordinary ship
Performing a very awesome task
While transporting lost souls
From the present and the past.

Deep within the heart of this
Soul-saving liner
Shines a bright and glowing light
Resting on a soft recliner.

When a soul comes in contact
With this ever present light,
Somehow it gains new hope
From this awe-inspiring sight.

It only takes one saving touch
To turn these souls around
And let them know with certainty
That they were lost, but now are found.

And so this ship of saving souls
Sails safely on it course
Reminding those who come on board
Of this divine and saving force.

# THE CANDLE ON THE CORNER

A lost soul faced intolerable odds
And witnessed hatred and crime.
He met dissension from negative attention,
This happened from time to time.

He encountered issues in society each day
And pressure from all of his peers.
He wanted to retreat and admit defeat
And hide his constant fears.

All seemed hopeless with nowhere to turn
These problems he could not handle,
But when all appeared dark, he noticed a spark
From a bright and glowing candle.

There it was, on a neglected corner
With nothing or anyone around.
As he drew near, he lost all fear;
He knew he was on special ground.

A voice from the candle gave him new hope
And offered him helpful advice.
"I will give you direction and divine protection,
If you believe in Jesus Christ."

From that day on, his life had changed
A light shone on his face;
He walked with pride with his personal guide
Who had blessed him with mercy and grace!

DEVOTIONAL THOUGHT:
*"For the Son of Man has come to save that which was lost."*
Matthew 18:11  NKJV

# MATCHING SHOES
## (Walking Through Time)

I open up my Bible and explore with great concern
The wonders of the Maker and all that I would learn.
There's excitement and adventure, which appeal to curious minds,
Reminding us the stories that are repeated countless times.
And as I walk through every page and see what God has done,
I feel the need to tag along and witness everyone.

Let's take a look at Moses who was duty bound by God
To lead his people from bondage with an ordinary rod.
And when he reached the open sea, he stretched the rod on high,
The Israelites were frightened now and Moses wondered 'Why'?
They knew that Pharaoh's army would kill them all for sure.
But Moses with his faith in God provided a mighty cure.
Myself, being in the crowd, I walked with grateful pride
And looked back on the waters when I reached the other side.
I thank my God for saving me as well as all the Hebrews
And gave me a chance to walk in consecrated shoes.

Moving on, we view the books where Jesus was involved
And see what miracles He performed and problems that He solved.
He often taught His followers to go where He would lead
Through faith and prayers and sacrifice, they would never want or need.
One incident involving faith was tested on the sea
A storm came up and shook the boat and caused anxiety.
The sea began to calm itself as Jesus did approach
While walking on the water for to save the rocking boat.
So as I grabbed onto His hand, we walked the ebbing tide,
I had no fear as we drew near—He was the perfect guide!

These incidents and wondrous stories written in the book
Gave me some inspiration as I took a second look.
They reminded me how awesome is our Father up above
For saving us from sin and shame with all His perfect love.

So as I close the holy book, I sit back and I smile,
I knew that when I opened it, I knew it was worthwhile!

DEVOTIONAL THOUGHT:
*"But these are written that you may believe that Jesus is the Christ,
The Son of God, and that believing you may have life in His name."*
John 20:31  NKJV

# THE WASHING MACHINE

There's an unusual washing machine
Which is truly, truly blessed
And it's always ready to cleanse the body
And give you peace and rest.

It's really good at what it does,
Believe it or not,
With its three running cycles,
It takes in a lot.

Bring all your dirty laundry
For the cleansing of your life.
It washes away the filthy stains
And all your stress and strife.

The agitation of the Spirit
Will leave you spotless clean,
Just add the right "detergent"
Into the washing machine.

No coins to start the cycle
As it modifies your soul,
It'll wash, rinse and spin---
As it prepares to make you whole.

And when the cycle is over,
You'll have a spiritual high;
You'll never know the difference
Until you really try!

DEVOTIONAL THOUGHT:
*"Behold, you desire truth in the inward parts, and in the hidden part, you will make me to know wisdom. Purge me with hyssop, and I shall be clean; wash me, and I shall be whiter than snow."*
Psalm 51:6-7   NKJV

# THE WIND

A blowing, gentle, whistling breeze
Streaks down from heavenly skies,
And quietly kisses the standing trees
While sweeping the countryside.

One mission is to cool the earth,
And to interrupt the heat;
And steal across the river's turf
While serving us relief.

This natural current of moving air
Is sometimes set in motion
And moves obediently on God's plan
Without a thought or notion.

It simply obeys the word of God
As it travels to and fro;
And demonstrates its might and strength,
When it's moving fast or slow.

Remember, that God surrounds you daily;
He is there through thick and thin.
He always shows his awesome power,
With His presence in the wind.

DEVOTIONAL THOUGHT:
*"So the men marveled, saying, 'Who can this be, that even
The winds and the sea obey Him?'"* Matthew 8:27 NKJV

# THE LIGHTHOUSE

There's a lighthouse in the distance
Near the rough and open sea--
A tower of majestic strength,
Watching over you and me.

It stands above the water's edge
And peers out on the ocean,
A vigil warning travelers
Of every shady motion.

It is genuine and awesome
As its beacon scans the night,
A reminder to the fearful few
Of its presence and its might.

When its guiding light appears,
It gives a joyous sign.
To let you know there is no fear
Of being left behind.

When you open up your heart to Christ
And let Him come within,
He'll be your ever guiding light
And lead you safe from sin!

DEVOTIONAL THOUGHT
*"I am the light of the world. He who follows Me shall not walk in darkness, but have the light of life."* John 8:12 NKJV

# THE WHEELBARROW

In a lonely woodshed on the outskirts of town
Stood an unusual wheelbarrow, solid and sound.
It was a blessed vehicle with gifts divine,
And filled with the spirit---one of a kind.

It was created with care and tender love
By the Master Designer from heaven above.
And when it traveled, it touched many lives
Giving instant support wherever it arrived.

It was awesome to see this wheelbarrow roll
Bringing comforting relief to the young and the old.
This wheelbarrow was noted for its divine appeal
As it moved very quietly on its leading wheel.

The wheel and the legs made the Trinity
The Father, the Son and the Holy Ghost made three.
The loads that were carried by this lowly wheelbarrow
Traveled far and near through streets wide and narrow.

And everywhere that wheelbarrow rolled,
Miraculous events would often unfold.
There was no secret what this wheelbarrow could do
To those sufferers who touched it and their bodies made new.

So often it appeared in the midst of a crowd
Where there were shouts of "Master" from humbled heads bowed.
Its care and concern were truly well known,
But in moments of silence, it was often alone.

There, in the bleakest darkness of day,
It sat silent and still and began to pray,
Reminding us clearly of the burdens it hauled,
As it dutifully answered its Father's call.
And when it had finished the work that it started,
Its mission---complete, it soon departed.

DEVOTIONAL THOUGHT:
*"Casting all your care upon Him, for He cares for you."*
1 Peter 5:7   NKJV

# CHAINS

In our daily lives, we encounter Satan
And sometimes we yield to sin;
He plays enticing games with his unholy chains
And pulls our souls within.

One chain that's used to destroy our minds
And keep us helpless and restricted.
They're uppers and downers---drugs that we frown on
And their destruction is often predicted.

There are other chains that affect us often
And make us rob and steal
Instead of contentment, there's envy and resentment,
These are chains that are tragic, but real.

Then there're chains of physical desire
And wanting another's spouse;
It may cause some pain with nothing to gain
Leaving one stranded and helpless with doubt.

But then there's a chance to break from Satan
By getting involved with Christ.
Just speak his name and break the chains,
And avoid any stress or strife.

With Christ in your life, the chains of Satan
Will forever be a thing of the past.
You'll avoid despair and then declare
My chains are broken at last!

# FLIGHT

Out of a world of darkness, my mind looks back
When Satan had me sign a pact.
Satan had taken over my soul
And showed that he was in control.

My mind was drunk with despair and vice;
I knew I'd forever pay a price.
He showed me a place of no return
Where sinners and wrongdoers would forever burn.

I viewed my life and staked my claim
And determined I'd break from sin and shame.
I felt my faith coming back again
And moving from this world of sin.

I regained my hope while leaving there
And sought my Lord with a fervent prayer.
As I clasped my hands to kneel and pray,
I asked my Lord to have his way.

Reach down and take me by my hand
And lead me from this sinful land.
Lord, open my eyes and clear my sight,
And give me wings to make my flight

While traveling briskly through the air,
I felt my comfort level there
And saw my Savior's smiling face
As I received his saving grace!

# HIJACKED

Watch out for Satan,
He's on a mission
To hijack your soul
Under any condition.

He'll feed you with words
That will smother your faith,
And leave you vulnerable,
And utterly disgraced.

He's an opportunist
Who is full of tricks;
Hijacking your soul
Is one of his risks.

You must renew your faith
In our Lord, Jesus Christ.
You will avoid sin and shame
And save your life!

# A.I.D.S.
## Advising Individuals Devoted to Satan

There comes a time in life
Where changes must be made.
The sinner will realize
That his debts must be paid.

Satan's a schemer and a liar;
He pulls you in with treats.
It's another fading tactic,
Without comfort or relief.

He takes the opportunity
To seize your idle mind
And offer you the world,
With goods of every kind.

He knows your every weakness,
And the things you like the most.
He serves you up with praises;
He's your complementary host.

But hear me as I tell you,
That all of this is wrong.
His genuine concern
Is based on stringing you along.

Don't listen to his speeches
Or anything he claims.
He'll take away your soul and more,
You'll never be the same.

By renewing your commitment
To your Father up above,
He will rescue you from sin and shame
With His everlasting love.

He will give you the tools
To fight off Satan and his ways,
With faith, prayer and sacrifice,
You will truly be amazed.

You need to get your life back,
And have complete peace within.
God will grant you happiness
While praising Him. Amen.

# C.I.A.
# (Christ In Action)

When you stand at the door and extend your hand
And you get joy and satisfaction,
It's your duty to greet and ultimately seat---
It's a gesture of Christ in action.

When you lift up your voice and sing to His glory
And you see there's joy in the crowd,
Just quicken your pace with a smile on your face
Be humble, be gracious, be proud.

When you open your Bible and prepare your text
And you have the congregation's attention
Just call on the Lord and you'll strike a chord,
They'll hang on every word you mention.

When you visit the sick and shut-in members
And your presence is welcomed by all
Just remember your tasks when someone asks
"Are you answering the Master's call?"

There's much to be said when we do our part
And allow Christ to intercede.
There's a blessed reaction from this positive action
From individuals having a need.

DEVOTIONAL THOUGHT:
*"I will bless the Lord at all times; His praise shall continually
Be in my mouth."* Psalm 34:1  NKJV

# D.O.C. 'J'
# (Depending On Christ) Jesus

Christ is the remedy for all of your problems
No matter how great or small.
Just state your claim and mention His name,
And He'll answer your every call.

If your heart is heavy from stress and strife
And you don't know which way to turn;
Christ has a prescription for every subscription,
And He fills them with love and concern.

If your body is racked with pain and disease
And there's no one else around,
Christ has the answer for this malignant "cancer",
He will pick you up when you're down.

Trust in Jesus, your friend and companion
He'll be your perfect guide.
The things He will do as He ministers to you
Will leave you beaming with pride!

DEVOTIONAL THOUGHT:
*"Come to Me, all you who labor and are heavy laden,
and I will give you rest. Take My yoke upon you and
learn from Me, for I am gentle and lowly in heart, and
you will find rest for your souls. For My yoke is easy
and My burden is light."* Matthew 11:28-30  NKJV

# MESSAGE IN A BOTTLE

There's a message in a bottle pulled from the bay
Jesus is coming, and He's on His way.
What have you done in your life thus far?
Is everything ready and up to par?

He's coming to claim what He promised He'd do.
Get your house in order, He's coming for you.
No need to get worried or stir up a fuss,
Just do what you have to, do what you must.

Will you recognize Him when He knocks on your door?
Will He be dressed as a king, or the lowly poor?
What will you say when He extends His hand?
Will you draw back in fear or take a stand?

If you've lived your life as you know you should,
You need not worry if you've done what you could.
Just read your scriptures and acknowledge His word;
Be patient and kind and continue to serve.

DEVOTIONAL THOUGHT:
*"Then the righteous will answer Him, saying, 'Lord,
when did we see You hungry and feed You, or thirsty
and give You drink? When did we see You a stranger
and take You in, or naked and clothe You? Or when
did we see You sick, or in prison, and come to You?
And the King will answer and say to them, 'Assuredly,
I say to you, inasmuch as you did it to one of the least
of these My brethren, you did it to Me.'"*
Matthew 25:37-40   NKJV

# CLEAN UP YOUR ACT
## (Jesus is Coming)

The time has come to make decisions
And get your life on track.
Don't hesitate or procrastinate
It's time to clean up your act.

Remember when you made a remark
And hurt another's feelings?
It was your intention to cause dissension,
Now it's time for confession and healing.

Another incident involved a test
And you stole the answers in advance.
No one knew, but it was up to you,
To come clean while you had the chance.

While attending church on Sunday morning
You held back on your tithes.
You came in late and ignored the plate,
And excused yourself with lies.

These incidents are just a few
To warn you from the start
It would be wise to open your eyes
And let Jesus into your heart!


DEVOTIONAL THOUGHT:
*"Therefore you also be ready, for the Son of Man is coming at an hour you do not expect."* Matthew 24:44
NKJV

# THE PASSION

Jesus was grabbed and went in peace
And questioned by others, with no relief.
He stood in a courtyard, silent and still
Obeying the voice of His Father's will.

Our Lord and Savior was judged by a crowd
A crown of thorns placed on his brow.
A wooden cross, he dragged along,
While being abused by an angry throng.
He endured forty lashes on His precious back,
Which was bruised and burning from this vicious attack.
He gritted His teeth while enduring the pain
From an angry whip which had nothing to gain.

He waged this battle and paid the cost
And surrendered his life on a wooden cross.
He was placed in a tomb, borrowed no less,
For two days His body remained at rest.

On the third day—to everyone's surprise,
He overcame death and did arise.
All were stunned it was plain to see,
Our Lord and Savior claimed a victory!

# THE REMORSEFUL THIEF

In the darkness of the hour
Jesus hung on the cross,
For a nameless crime,
He was paying the cost.

Thirsting and aching,
He shouldered the pain.
His free flowing blood
Left a crimson stain.

During this hour of darkness,
Two others were there
One on either side,
An ungodly pair.

Two thieves were accused
Of unnamed crimes,
Facing their fate
On borrowed time.

One thief was remorseful
For the sins he had done;
The other was merciless
Against God's only Son.

The remorseful thief
Was assured by Christ
That this day he would join Him
In Paradise!

DEVOTIONAL THOUGHT:

*Then one of the criminals who were hanged blasphemed Him, saying, "If You are the Christ, save Yourself and us." But the other, answering, rebuked him, saying, "Do you not even fear God, seeing you are under the same condemnation? And we indeed justly, for we receive the due reward of our deeds; Then he said to Jesus, "Lord remember me when You come into Your kingdom." And Jesus said to him, "Assuredly, I say to you, today You will be with Me in Paradise."* Luke 23:39-43 NKJV

# THE PARTY

There's a party tonight, bring your invitation
Come one, come all to this great celebration.
Sinners and Saints, all are invited.
It's a party for Jesus, no one will be slighted.

B.Y.O.B – bring your own Bible,
We're going to praise His name with this joyous revival.
There'll be things to do and plenty of food
As we enjoy the occasion of this festive mood.

Tell Isaac and Jacob to come to the feast
And join in the praises of this special treat.
Remind Joseph to come and bring David along,
We'll interpret some dreams and sing some songs.

There'll be many surprises and miraculous events
Coming from the gospels in the New Testament.
Everything has been planned and ready to start
Clear out your mind and open up your heart.

When all is over and the party is done,
Remember this day that was filled with fun.
Your life will be new and filled with love
With rewarding gifts from the Father above.

DEVOTIONAL THOUGHT:
*"Then he said to his servants, 'The wedding is ready, but those who were invited were not worthy. Therefore, go into the highways, and as many as you find, invite to the wedding.' So the servants went out into the highways and gathered together all whom they found, both bad and good. And the wedding hall was filled with guests."*
Matthew 22:8-10   NKJV

# THE SHEPHERD IN THE STICKS

There is a little country church
Straight down the unpaved road
Where sinners and the weary-worn
Drop off their heavy loads.

This sanctuary in the sticks
Requires no special prayer.
Its purpose is to save the souls
And heal the bodies there.

The preacher has the awesome task
Of  providing spiritual food.
To help the lost recover fast,
And change their sinful moods.

One thing about this country preacher
One hasn't noticed yet
Is the way he handles everyone
Without getting them upset.

He has an easy manner
That is passionate and kind,
And when you try to question him,
He truly doesn't mind.

When sinners listen to his words
They know they are for real.
Then he has a gentle touch
That makes the body heal.

So as you travel down this road
With burdens now and then,
Remember that this man of God
Will gladly take you in!

DEVOTIONAL THOUGHT:
The Lord is my Shepherd; I shall not want. He makes Me to lie down in green pastures; He leads me beside the still waters. He restores my soul; Psalm 23:1-3a NKJV

# CHURCH FOLK: PASS THE PLATE!

Each Sunday as the church doors open
The church folk enter in,
And quickly take their treasured seats
As the day's service begins.

The women are dressed in vivid colors
With hair and hats in place.
The men are suited down, you see,
As curiosity greets each face.

They're wondering what the preacher has
In store for them today.
He's used to preaching to the lights,
With nothing more to say.

Somewhere amidst the droning words
A thought will strike a chord.
A chorus of 'Amens' are heard
When he thinks the folks are bored.

Message over, and the plate is passed
As the begging preacher pleads,
"Give all you have to the Lord today,"
Then he takes his seat---relieved.

"Quiet money is what we need
(As he drops a dollar in),
The church folk listened to what he said,
And 'quietly' responded then.

"These penny-pinching folk in here
Will let the church go down.
The Lincoln coins that strike the plate
Have made an awful sound!"

Yes, church folk have a way with words
When responding to the Lord
But, they expect to go to heaven
And receive their just reward!

DEVOTIONAL THOUGHT:
*"Will a man rob God? Yet you have robbed Me!*
*But you say, 'In what way have we robbed You?'*
*In tithes and offerings."* Mal. 3:8  NKJV

# CHURCH FOLK: CHURCH MEETING

Ever so often, the church will meet
To hear from the congregation
An agenda is set to discuss some issues
Without conflict or trepidation.

The floor is opened by the church's pastor
And the church folk are asked to speak.
"There's a homeless man, who visited here,
Who unknowingly took my seat!"

The pastor is concerned about this issue
And quickly makes a remark,
He sees Miss Bessie is agitated
From listening to her bark!

"Now, Miss Bessie, I've heard your complaint
And certainly it's obviously clear,
You have no legitimate gripe, I see,
But, is that person here?"

A homeless man came quietly forward
A crown of thorns he wore
His bleeding hands were by his side
As he stood within the door.

The church folk watched him in the aisle
They believed not what they saw.
His altered look and gentle words
Left them in spiritual awe.

Then he quietly left the church
And vanished out the door.
The church folk remained filled with guilt,
But they saw him no more.

"You never know," the preacher said
When the Savior comes within.
Prepare your hearts to receive Him now,
While there is time. Amen."

# THE CHRISTIAN SOLDIER

He's off to war in a foreign land
Making this sacrifice and taking a stand.
Rehearsing his thoughts of friends back home,
Reminding himself, he's now on his own.

He must keep focused and ever aware
Of hostile fire from the enemy there;
And make the decisions to do what he must,
While fighting the foe from dawn to dusk.

A badge of courage he'll wear on his heart
And increase his faith while doing his part.
He'll be fighting this war, miles from home,
But, this Christian soldier will not be alone.

He'll keep in his backpack the Holy Bible,
A guiding light for strength and survival.
He'll steal away when the time is right
And talk to his Father in the middle of the night.

His words will be simple, a divine request
To keep him safe, in a war he detests.
And give him the knowledge of facing the fact,
Faith in the Almighty will bring him back.

He's made up his mind after talking with the Lord
To face the challenge of going abroad.
So, now he's gone to this foreign place
With God on his side and a smile on his face.

# SIGNS

Some man-made signs take control of our lives
And they're only for our protection,
There're signs on the street, which we often mistreat,
But they try to give us direction.

The yield sign is posted to make you aware
Of oncoming traffic in view,
While you're driving along, and you're in the wrong,
If an accident occurs, it's on you.

Then there're signs with a posted speed limit,
They're to keep your driving in check,
If you ignore these signs, you might be fined,
Or, worse, end up in a wreck.

Some other signs involve our souls,
And the way we live each day.
Just look for the scripture, it'll paint you a picture
Of reasons you shouldn't delay.

Christ is coming, will you be ready?
He's prepared a way for you.
Heed the signs and avoid the fines,
It's a charge that you must do.

# MY PRAYER

I make no excuses for the things I've done
For the problems I've caused for everyone.
My head is aching from thoughts of guilt
And the many lies I've overbuilt.

I want a chance to right my wrongs
And change the ones I've brought along.
I lost faith in God and gone astray,
And lost the desire to kneel and pray.

I ask my God to change my soul,
And make me right before I'm old
And just maybe give me one more chance
Before I take my final stance.

I often wish I could change my past,
But this would be an awesome task.
So as I travel the road of deception,
I truly want to regain acceptance,
And turn my life from sin and shame,
And restore my dignity and my name.

Lord, let me speak while I am here
There are certain things I must make clear.
Lord, let me live the best I can
According to what you have planned.

Please lead me down a righteous path
Avoiding sin and Satan's wrath.
So as I retrace my road from sin,
I'll renew my faith in You. Amen

# LITTLE THINGS

In life, we move at a steady pace
And forget the little things
That support the road to happiness,
And the comfort that they bring.

We fail to make a compliment
One that means so much,
And proper words we fail to use,
That add a special touch.

In our haste to visit shut-in friends
We often leave from there,
And hurry to our destination
Without a song or prayer.

If God can raise you from your sleep
And protect you in many ways,
It should always be the fitting thing
To give Him all the praise.

For if you think these words and deeds
Won't cure a troubling soul,
Someone will always remember well
How your kindness made them whole.

# LABOR OF LOVE

When I see what God has created,
      I've always been aware
Of the beauty of His precious trees,
      And all His flowers there.
Each plant has a different story
      Of how it came to be,
Standing tall and stately
      As His pines and shrubbery.
These wonders that have stood the time
      While bathing in the sun
Have come to be a blessing
      As I see what God has done.
No matter what the season is,
      They're always standing fair
Ever under watchful eyes,
      And my Father's constant care.
When I look at all the creations
      That have blossomed by His hand,
Then I truly appreciate
      And fully understand!

# IN THE COUNTRY

The early dawn descending dew
Creeps over the sleeping grass,
And eagerly opens up the day
To reveal the sun at last.

The sweetness of the mountain air
Comes gently down on me,
I awaken in the summer breeze
Out in the country.

As I look around the countryside
And the grandeur of the land,
I know it was a work of art
From God's master plan.

The colorful flowers open up
As the birds begin to chirp,
Revealing faithfully to you and me
God's awesome handiwork.

The pine, oak, spruce and maple
Stretch forth their leafy arms
In response to God's constant calling
Out near the country farms.

In the awakened day, the insects crawl
Over flowers and shrubbery;
And the bees are flitting from plant to plant
Out in the country.

And so I start my day with joy,
The Spirit is guiding me,
I've seen the Father's smiling face,
Out in the country!

# I'LL BE SATISFIED

When the world is rid of Satan and sin
And prejudice is put aside,
When children respect their parents and kin,
Then I'll be satisfied.

When war is just a thing of the past
And fighting will be denied,
When terrorists stop their killing at last
Then I'll be satisfied.

When teachers get the materials they need
And kids view learning with pride,
When educators do their best to succeed,
Then I'll be satisfied.

When dealers stop abusing drugs
And hookers turn the tide,
When young men cease to be a "thug",
Then I'll be satisfied.

These challenging thoughts and wishes here
Will help us all decide
To deal with each one's pain and fear,
Then we'll all be satisfied.

# IT NEVER CROSSED MY MIND

I would have awakened the world today,
But I forgot to set the time.
I would have fed the horses hay,
But it never crossed my mind.

I wanted to acknowledge the shape of things
And people left in a bind.
I know what consequences bring,
But it never crossed my mind.

Somewhere a thought has passed me by,
Could this be by design?
Somewhere a plan has gone awry,
But it never crossed my mind.

I desired to know the penitent thief
Next to my Lord Divine
And somehow offer him relief,
But it never crossed my mind.

Lastly, I turned my life around,
This was a positive sign.
I was lost, but now am found,
This certainly crossed my mind!

# CHALLENGES

Lately I've been thinking
       About the shape the world is in
And how I'd like to give my life
       Some meaning without sin.
I had a fleeting thought today
       Of how to pass the time,
There're many things I'd like to do
       Before my life declines.
One thing I'd like to do right now
       Before I leave this earth
Is having someone teach me
       How to swim and how to surf.
Then I'd like to fantasize
       And go out and pretend
To grab onto a butterfly net
       And catch a powerful wind.
Or face two menacing bulls
       During a Mexican bullfight,
Then grab a mighty eagle
       By its wings while still in flight.
Another is to take a chance
       And climb a mountainside
And feel the satisfaction
       Of knowing I had tried.
Lastly, I would like to see
       The Master's smiling face
And know that I can count on Him,
       His mercy and His grace!

# BEYOND THE OPEN SEA

My life is filled with ups and downs
A tribute to reality.
I take a pause to plead my cause,
So others may hear my plea.

I feel the need to tell someone
I'll do it openly,
And use my right to view my plight
Beyond the open sea.

I lost my job when times were good
Why did this happen to me?
There's a better life without stress or strife
Beyond the open sea.

I thought about my relatives
And all my family,
There was much concern from what I learned
Beyond the open sea

And then I prayed to my Father above,
Who answered me faithfully;
You'll gain insight with Jesus Christ,
Beyond the open sea!

# Family/Relations

# BEFORE THE FLOOD

There is much to do before the flood,
And get everything in order.
There's anticipation of devastation
From impending stormy waters.

The weather forecasts cloudy skies
With a tragic burst of rain.
We made a plan to leave this land
And never return again.

Alarms were sounded and notices posted
For preparing to leave this place.
"Grab all that you can in each of your hands,
Go quickly, and safely with haste!"

The heavens darkened as the storm approached,
A cascade of water came down.
There was no surprise from the angry skies,
There was destruction all around.

My family was safe from the raging storm;
We gave a thankful prayer.
I thank my Master for avoiding disaster
When He showed how much He cared.

# THESE TIMES

In this world of chaos, doubt and confusion
There's much to be said today.
No religion in schools or counterfeit rules
These concerns are here to stay.

There are constant thefts and terrorist threats
While gangs will kill anyone
Dissension is rising and families realizing
Their greatest fear is the gun.

Many lives are lost and we pay the cost
With fear from violent crimes
There's a need for renovation for this present generation
We're living in dangerous times.

Drugs are rampant on every corner
Using children as a primary source
Their lives---incomplete when they die on the streets
And there's never relief or remorse.

Arsonists and vandals have plagued the scene
And constantly hide from view
There's daily frustration from senseless violations
Inflicted upon me and you.

If there are going to be changes made,
They have to start with you.
Just change your style while raising your child
And renew your attitude, too.

# THE PROMISE

Long ago, when I was a child,
I would retreat to my room and play;
One could hear the noise from my broken toys,
It was what I did each day.

There were times when Mama didn't work
And we shared a slice of bread;
But I remember the words, which I often heard,
"Don't worry, you will be fed."

My dad had left when I was small
So we had to make ends meet;
Sometimes I'd wonder, if we'd go under,
But Mom wouldn't accept defeat.

I helped my mom in many ways
And at the age of ten,
I went about with my paper route,
On me she would often depend.

As times went on, she changed her job
And things were much better by far;
She gained a promotion with her punctual devotion
And bought a brand new car.

It was God's grace and His tender mercy
That finally brought us through;
My mom would pray each and every day,
And I would kneel beside her, too.

She asked our Heavenly Father above
To keep us free from sin,
And protect us now, and show us how,
This was our prayer. Amen.

# THE JAR

When I was young my father left
To go and fight the war.
He said my son you're growing up,
Here's something by the door.

He pointed to an odd-shaped jar,
He'd fashioned with his hands.
He filled it almost to the top
Mixed in with dirt and sand.

He ordered me to take a spoon
And remove some mix each day,
And make sure I stored it in a bag
While he was gone away.

"This war is something I detest,
I hate to leave my home,
And fight the foe in a foreign land
Leaving your mom and you alone."

As time went on the first two years
Were very hard on us.
I knew that fighting in the war,
Dad considered it unjust.

Then one day we got a letter,
It had a certain seal.
It was a message from my father,
A message that was real.

I read the letter to my mom
And gave her all the facts.
Dad had written it before he died,
Before he was attacked.

In the bottom of the hand-made jar
Amidst the dirt and sand
There was a security banker's key,
With instructions and a plan.

My father loved his family so
He knew we had to survive.
The money that was in the bank
Would keep us both alive.

And so we thank him for his plans,
In a letter from afar;
A treasure that would keep us safe,
From the bottom of a jar!

# A MISSING SON

Wars and fighting, they take their toll
As young men battle to reach a goal.
In a foreign land, our enemies don't care,
Destruction and killing are everywhere.

The burden is born by families back home
Where daily reports lists the dead and unknown.
Mothers are heartbroken and fathers are grieving
About a senseless war and their sons' leaving.

The cries continue from tear-stained eyes
Of broken families when someone dies.
Young men sacrificing, and not yet twenty-one;
They're someone's brother and someone's son.

They're fighting a war against an undaunted foe,
Fearful, and not knowing which way to go.
They protect our country at any cost.
We mourn their deaths when their lives are lost.

Bombs are dropping and children are dying,
Families destroyed and kinfolk are crying.
When the smoke has cleared, and the battle is won,
Someone counts the loss of a missing son.

# FATHER TO SON

Wake up, my son, and open your eyes
The world is looking at YOU.
You're going through a phase and are set in your ways,
And traveling the wrong path, too.

Our young men are dying from violence and hatred
You have a choice to make.
When you approach the scene of a dying teen
It's more than one can take.

Who's filling your head with dangerous thoughts
And giving you deceitful advice?
You need salvation with God and education,
These supports will strengthen your life.

Pull up your pants and comb your head,
And look for a new direction.
Start doing good in your neighborhood,
And help those needing protection.

It's never too late to change bad habits
And develop some positive ones.
Get rid of drug dealers and deceitful healers
And assault weapons—knives and guns.

Establish a foundation filled with the spirit
And invite God into your heart.
Help someone today, who's gone astray,
And rejoice in doing your part.

Remember these words and all that I tell you
As you travel the road of life.
Open your Bible for strength and survival,
And avoid temptation and strife!

DEVOTIONAL THOUGHT: Proverbs 1-3   NKJV

# BE A MAN

It's time to put away childish things
Accept responsibility, for whatever it brings.
As you grow older, you'll understand
It's time to wake up and be a man.

Sometimes it's hard to see the light
With good upbringing, you'll be all right.
Lay out your future, and follow your plans,
Be not dismayed, just be a man.

Avoid narcotics and illegal drugs,
Criminals, thieves and wanna-be thugs.
Do what's right, I know you can,
Just don't forget to be a man.

Be kind and gentle to those you love,
Be thankful for the blessings from your Father above.
Remember your duties when you're in demand.
You'll gain respect for being a man.

Others will recognize the things you've done,
And the many hassles you've overcome.
They'll praise your name and shake your hand,
And proudly announce---there goes a man!

# THE ENCOUNTER

When we first met, many years ago,
In a college eating place,
A spark ignited deep within,
And my heart began to race.

I locked my eyes upon her smile
And stared across the table;
I tried to say a word or two,
But found I wasn't able.

Suddenly, I felt my nerves on edge
And decided to make my move;
I quickly introduced myself
With a different attitude.

We talked awhile on many things
And things we liked to do.
I wanted to ask her out sometimes,
But my words were slow and few.

Suddenly, I mustered up the courage
To ask her for a date.
I hadn't met her family yet,
So, I was told I had to wait.

As time went on, we became engaged
And eventually tied the knot.
Memories of our first encounter,
I never, ever forgot.

# FIRST DATE

Today was the day I planned so long,
I knew that nothing would ever go wrong.
I checked myself and splashed my cologne,
Then called her on the telephone.
But when I approached the moment of truth,
I suddenly felt----alone and aloof.
My heart was throbbing hard and fast.
I wanted this time to quickly pass.
The roses I clutched were falling down,
Their petals were spread all over the ground.
I straightened my tie and wiped my brow,
I wanted to retreat---especially now.
Sweaty palms and feet to match,
I wondered if I'd ever win this catch.
She opened the door and stood in awe--
Amazed and pleased at what she saw.
I said to myself, 'This is great!'
No one would believe---this <u>WAS</u> my first date.

# INTERVENTION

When I first met you, I was drawn to your beauty,
There was much I did admire;
I would hold your hand and be the man,
This <u>WAS</u> my true desire.

We went many places and did many things,
We were perfect for each other;
I suddenly realized, when I opened my eyes,
That <u>YOU</u> were close to another.

My eyes were cloudy; I was losing your love,
I knew there was nothing to save me.
There were so many clues for me to choose,
I felt you were going to trade me.

I prayed a prayer to my Lord above
For I felt that you had betrayed me.
You made up your mind; you had a new find,
I knew you were going to trade me.

When I first met you, you swayed me.
It was your intent to get me, and so you played me.
When you got tired, you betrayed me.
Now it's your desire to trade me.

My heavenly Father had answered my prayers
Your love no longer enslaved me.
You broke my heart, but I made a new start,
For my faith in God had saved me.

Your love had depraved me,
But my faith had saved me.
I knew you had betrayed me,
But God's love had saved me!

# THE JADED MASK

Sometimes in life we're disillusioned
      About happiness and utter confusion.
We hide our thoughts and shield our eyes,
      Finding comfort in a new disguise.
And put on a face that's not our own,
      Pretending that we are not alone.
A constant smile hides our frown,
      And others never suspect we're down.
They only see the outer appearance,
      Not realizing there's been interference.
Our secret's safe and remains concealed
      The true feelings are never revealed.
This tragic deceit--we practice for years,
      Continuously duping our inner fears.
This is such an awesome task,
      Keeping up this jaded mask.

# MORNING MATTERS

What concerns me most as I rise and shine
Is the restless sleep I leave behind.
I toss and turn all through the night,
And wake up to my bed's delight.

It seems I'm being ganged upon
Before the rising of the sun.
This calls for patience and a plan,
My bed has gained the upper hand.

It seems at night it comes alive
And racks my body with its jive.
This nightmare is my main concern,
Attacking me in every turn.

No wonder when I wake to rise
Sleepy bags have claimed my eyes.
And when I think I'd win the war,
It then returns to fight some more.

Tables turned--- I've had enough.
It's time to show this bed my stuff.
Tonight I'm going to stay awake
And gladly give this bed a shake.

For now, I'll take a noonday nap,
And get up late to set my trap.
This blasted bed I do abhor,
I think I'll nail it to the floor.
And when I've given this bed a fright,
Then I'll sleep throughout the night!

# Making A Difference

# THE VERSATILE LADY

In a town down South in the Carolinas
There's a story about a woman of merit.
She is truly endowed, and it makes me proud,
To know that I can share it.

She has many brothers and several sisters,
She goes by the name of Tina.
With a smile on her face, she's easy to trace,
You'll know what I mean when you've seen her.

She's a beautiful lady with a gracious spirit,
And a prominent walk to match.
With caramel skin and a seductive grin
She's certainly a promising catch.

She's caring and loving, though sometimes stubborn,
And possesses a heart of gold.
If you've ever met her, you'll never forget her,
She's unique and wholly in control.

Versatility describes her many skills
No task is too great or too small.
She puts in her time as she successfully climbs,
She has an answer for every call.

Whether teaching children or working alone
Or driving her busy car,
She has the potential, which is really essential
And surpasses others by far.

Yes, here is a queen—knowledgeable and sweet
And determined to do her best.
She sets her limits and is never timid,
She does it with incredible zest.

# MR. IGGADEE

In a southern town, where the cotton grows,
There arrived a mystery;
Of a strange man with a crooked hand---
He was called Mr. Iggadee.

He was big and round and walked with a limp,
His awkwardness made him slow;
When folks saw him coming, and the tune he was hummin'
They knew he would put on a show.

He loved attention and the crowds would gather
To see him dance and play;
With his harmonica in hand, he was a one-man band,
And he did it most every day.

He was a spiritual person, and the folks knew well
He didn't have much to say,
But when he came out, the people would shout,
And then he would begin to play.

His music was magic, it had powers to heal
And the sick and the dying came around;
Their bodies became whole as it reached their souls,
They responded to every sound.

One day he was gone, and no one knew
That he went the way that he came;
And the folks had no clue as to what they could do,
This town would never be the same.

# *THE BALLAD OF THE DUMMY - PT 1

A mighty tree was splintered down
Carved and shaped with extra care
Taking the form of a hollow head
And covered with black coarse hair.

The hands and arms, legs and feet
Were sewn to a hollow frame
With curious eyes and a draw string mouth,
Remorseful was his name.

His life was very complicated
While working every day,
For when it was his time to speak,
He had nothing good to say.

It seems it was his operator
Whose personality
Was split in two offensive ways,
So he spoke defiantly.

And when he moved the dummy's lips
He made a desperate plea,
What he said was out of line,
But he did it constantly.

So now you know the operator,
A man who wasn't well,
He ran his mouth incessantly
And ended up in jail.

The dummy that was made of wood
Went on the road alone,
You see it was his plan at first
To travel on his own!

# *THE BALLAD OF THE DUMMY – PT 2

When last we saw Remorseful
He had made it on his own.
He worked the comedy circuit
And built a beautiful home.

As time went on, he saw a chance
To make it to the top.
Laryngitis claimed his voice,
So his shows began to flop.

He thought about the operator
Who built him out of wood,
He wanted to get him out of jail,
But he wasn't sure he could.

He went to see the operator
And begged him pleadingly,
"I'll make a deal to bail you out,
But you must be my remedy."

So the operator said he would
And gladly took the deal
Getting out of jail and back to work
Gave him an instant thrill.

They started on the road again
The two of them were chummy,
The operator signed a pact,
And **HE** became the dummy!

# THE EMPATHETIC DUMMY

Some years have passed and the operator is old
But his wooden dummy is the same
While on the road the dummy carried the load
And eventually made a name.

The wooden dummy, which had switched his place,
Was worried about his health
His friend was weak; he had reached his peak,
And was feeling pity for himself.

So the dummy devised a viable plan
To encourage his friend along
He suggested a home for his friend to roam
Where he could do no wrong.

But the operator had other plans
He would not be confined this way,
He made up his mind to bide his time
Until his dying day.

So his partner, the dummy, took him in
And nourished him patiently.
He stayed with his friend until the end
He was his constant company.

*NOTE: The Ballad of the Dummy parts 1 and 2 were taken from my first book and included here as part of the continuing story of the Dummy.

# Bible Heroes & Heroines

# ORDINARY FOLK

There are kings, queens and wealthy folk
Who populate the land.
They want for nothing more in life
Than what they can command.

Then there are the other folk
Who live from day to day.
They work in ordinary jobs
With ordinary pay.

There lives are filled with ups and downs
And happy times at best;
They're determined to make the most in life
With things they can address.

Somewhere, somehow, sometime in life
These simple folk will rise
And take their worthy positions
Without trouble or disguise.

They'll rise above the riches
And above those who command
They'll proudly take their places
For they'll be in demand.

Let us take a look at David
Who fought Goliath alone;
He approached without armor,
But with only five smooth stones.

This lowly shepherd boy,
Who was truly divinely led,
Released a stone from his slingshot
And struck Goliath in the head.

The giant fell to earth
And when all was said and done,
This ordinary shepherd
Had the enemy on the run.

There are many stories in the book
On ordinary folk
Who rise above adversities
And give us all some hope.

When you're feeling down and out
And need a lift for sure,
Just open up your Bible,
It's the ever ready cure!

# THE STORM

Years ago, when the world was new,
And the people populated the land;
It was noted then that they lived in sin,
So God raised his mighty hand.

God was so angry that He made up His mind
That everything on earth must die.
But He searched the land and found one man
On whom He could truly rely.

Noah and his family were spared by God,
Because they were trying to be good.
God made it clear that the end was near,
And to build an ark of wood.

"I will flood the earth and kill all evil
And start all over again;
Take two of each kind, leave the rest behind,
They'll be safe and secure within."

So Noah was obedient and built the ark
And gathered two of each kind.
And God looked at the land and raised His hand,
It was only a matter of time.

For forty days and forty nights
The sky poured forth the rain.
The earth was cleansed of wickedness and sins
But the ark and Noah remained.

Finally, the skies were clearing up,
But the earth was filled with water.
Six months Noah waited as the waters abated,
THIS was God's divine order.

So, God told Noah to free the animals
Because the land had dried.
He released the pairs with thankful prayers
It was nothing he had to decide.

God made a promise with a rainbow sign
That he would never flood the earth again.
Noah gave a shout as the sun came out,
And the earth was on the mend.

DEVOTIONAL THOUGHT:
Genesis 6-9   NKJV

# THE ROADSIDE SHACK

On a starlit night on the outskirts of town
A star shone truly bright.
Wise men watched the sky, with a curious eye,
This <u>WAS</u> an awesome sight.

The star shone brightly o'er this shack
As the lowing of cattle were heard.
When the three came close, there was a heavenly host,
Evidence of the Master's word.

There was talk of one who would save the world
Could this be a welcome sign?
When they approached the back of this roadside shack
They wondered what they would find.

A magnificent sight greeted the three
When they peered inside the place.
Their eyes were open as they were hoping,
This was the sign of His Grace.

When they entered the front of this open shack
There was evidence of plenty good news.
The babe inside was the couple's pride
For He <u>WAS</u> the King of the Jews!

A host of angels surrounded the place
Where the lowly manger stood.
It was filled with straw as those who saw
Drew close to this crib of wood.

A glorious light encircled His head
And the Wise men knew this sign.
It was clear to them that this precious gem
Was our Lord and Savior divine.

As they made their way into the night,
Their hearts were filled with joy.
They felt redeemed from what they'd seen,
Concerning this baby boy.

They traveled across the countryside
Sharing what they had seen;
And brought the word to those who heard
About the newborn king!

DEVOTIONAL THOUGHT:
Matthew 2:1-12   NKJV

# THE ROD

In the land of Egypt where the Pharaohs ruled,
God's chosen people were kept;
There was no flight from this awful plight,
This was something they had to accept.

Year in and year out they endured the bondage
And almost gave up all hope;
They often complained with nothing to gain,
They were at the end of their rope.

But their prayers were answered in the days ahead,
The Lord had heard their cries;
There was a positive sign when one of their kind
Came forth with a complete surprise.

His name was Moses, born a Hebrew,
Who was found by an Egyptian queen;
He grew up wise under an Egyptian guise,
This was the ultimate dream.

The Israelites thought he was of Egyptian birth
They couldn't believe what they'd heard;
But he renounced his kingdom when he had seen them
And was moved and utterly disturbed.

He was banished from this land of riches
His name was nowhere to be spoken;
He was left to roam from this place called "home,"
He was tattered, torn and broken.

As he wandered aimlessly in the desert
He prayed to his Lord above;
To give him strength and confidence
And insurmountable love.

The Hebrew cloak and rod he carried
Before they cast him out;
Was well received in this time of need,
And comforted him, too, no doubt.

As time went on he met a woman
And the two of them were married,
And this voice of love came down from above,
In this land where he had tarried.

It spoke to Moses where he had stood
And told him to take off his shoes,
For all around was holy ground,
And spoke of the enslavement of the Jews.

Moses was ordered to return to Egypt
And to let the Pharaoh know,
God was truly disturbed and had given His word
"To let my people go!"

When Moses returned to the land of Egypt,
His brother accompanied him, too
He raised the rod that was blessed by God,
And spoke these words so true.

"My God has spoken and sent me here
And I want to let you know,
From this very day, I'm here to say,
'To let my people go!'"

Pharaoh's heart was heavily hardened
And he decided to disobey God,
Moses received his order and touched the water
With his newly blessed rod.

As time went on Pharaoh had not changed
And endured the many afflictions,
When he lost his son, he was truly outdone,
And decided to lift the restrictions.

When the Israelites were freed, they praised their God
They had waited for this day to arrive.
They took all they had, and were certainly glad,
They were weary, but safe and alive.

As they approached the sea, Moses raised the rod,
And the waters obeyed the Master;
They received ample protection from Divine direction,
And were safe from all harm and disaster.

As the waters parted from Divine obedience
The people were moving with haste.
Moses walked with pride as their leader and guide,
This was a test of their faith.

The Egyptians were stunned at this awesome sight,
They couldn't believe their eyes;
It wasn't their desire to be stopped by the fire,
This was a complete surprise!

After the Israelites had crossed the waters
There was joy and praises to God.
Moses returned the waters from Divine orders,
With the help of his blessed rod!

DEVOTIONAL THOUGHT:
Exodus chaps. 2-15  NKJV

# HAGAR - by Annel C. Cooke

An Egyptian slave,
She stood all alone
Living a life she could not call her own
Her mistress out of desperation
Forced her into an ugly situation
Got pregnant by Abraham to produce an heir,
Sarah got mad and ran her out of there.
Alone and miserable in the woods
God spoke to Hagar and promised to make good.
A nation I will make out of your precious son
He'll get his blessings, though he's not the promised son.
Go back to your mistress and endure for a time
I promised to bless you, I am God, I cannot lie
The promised son Isaac soon did arrive
But this was not one happy family of five.
Sarah had had it up to here
She told Abe to "cast that bondwoman and boy out of here!"
Back in the wilderness, her cry in distress
God spoke once again, "Hagar, I said I would bless!"
Just like from the spring of water He supplied,
He promised a nation from Ishmael to be multiplied
Trust Me in My Words, and rest in Me
Stand on my promises, and let it be!!

DEVOTIONAL THOUGHT:
Genesis chap. 16 (The story is told) and chap. 21
NKJV

# RUTH'S RAP - by Annel C. Cooke

Hey Ruth!
Yes Mom,
You've got some work to do
I'm going to get you noticed
By this rich related Jew
Now follow my plan
Listen carefully to me
This plan, if it works
Will make delight with glee!
Go out in the fields and glean like you've been doing
Remain that humble woman you are
Girl, my plan don't ruin!!
Now, keep it very righteous,
Get noticed by Boaz
The virtuous woman you're called
With spiritual pizzazz
Get him to fill this role
To carry on hubby's name
And make me a happy woman
Who can erase this shame!
Daughter, my dear, this is the plan
And if all turns out well,
You'll have another man!!

DEVOTIONAL THOUGHT:
Read the entire book of Ruth (chaps. 1-4) NKJV

# Tributes

# GOD'S CHOSEN FLOWER
## (In memory of Claudia Y. Bullock)

There's a rose in a garden of beautiful flowers
That was nurtured with tender love.
She was plucked from the earth, where she was given birth,
And now rests with her Father above.

She was such a very loving person,
Her living was truly worthwhile.
If you ever met her, you would not forget her,
Not even her beautiful smile.

Weep not for her, she's smiling now,
She's safe from suffering and pain.
She was much admired, no more is required,
She has nothing to prove or gain.

Her memory will live on with family and friends
And loved ones she's left behind.
We'll share the grief and offer relief
This moment, this place, this time.

# TRIBUTE TO REV. AND SIS. AUSTIN – S.T.A.R.S.

How many of you are familiar with a show entitled: **STAR SEARCH**? On this show, there are contestants who compete against one another for top billing. The winner goes on to compete against in-coming contestants on the next show, trying to maintain his position, hoping to move to the final level and on to a major contract in show business. Over seventeen years ago, there was a vacancy in the pulpit, and there was a search going on to fill this vacancy. For seventeen years now, we've been blessed with two super-stars in our midst who have worked diligently to win lost souls to Christ. They adopted the motto, "Come grow with us and establish a blessed family". When you start making comparisons, whom can you compare them with? Unlike one dimensional couples such as:

Ozzie/Harriet, Fred/Wilma, Homer/Marge, Desi/Luci, George/Weezie, Archie Bunker/ Edith.

They are multi-dimensional, and have not gone into syndication. As a matter of fact, you can see them live and in living color here at Emmanuel – year round. Well, what can I say about them? They are stylish, unselfish, versatile, and hard-working servants for the Lord. Now you ask what makes them so unique? First of all, they are **STARS**:

**S**ervants **T**aking **A**ctive **R**oles **S**eriously,   and

**S**incerely **T**rying to **A**ttract **R**esponsible **S**ervants

In the book of Matt., chap. 4:13, Jesus starts gathering his disciples. Likewise, our stars
gathered those members to help carry out the mission of the church.

**S**hepherds **T**ending **A**nd **R**escuing **S**heep

In Matt.9:36, (KJV) When Jesus saw the multitudes, he was moved with compassion on them, because they fainted, and were scattered abroad, as sheep having no shepherd. Likewise, our stars have come to be shepherds, to show lost sheep how to avoid the pitfalls of life.

## **S**aints **T**rying to **A**ctively **R**ebuke **S**atan

In Luke 4:8 (KJV), And Jesus answered and said unto him, "Get thee behind me, Satan: for it is written, thou shalt worship the Lord thy God, and him only shall thou serve. Here again, our shepherds have been faithfully getting the word out that Satan is a liar and a deceiver who is not to be trusted or received. They emphasize serving God only.

## **S**ervants **T**aking **A**im at **R**esistant **S**ouls

In the book of James 5:19-20, Brethren, if any of you do err from the truth, and one convert him; Let him know, that he which converteth the sinner from the error of his way shall save a soul from death, and shall hide a multitude of sins. Clearly the person who has slipped away is a believer who has fallen into sin—one who is no longer living a life consistent with his beliefs. Once again, at every opportunity, our stars extend the invitation to come to Jesus Christ. For so many years, they've been involved, and they're still involved today.

# TRIBUTE TO PASTOR & SIS. AUSTIN– MAY 2004

Ladies and gents, it's that time again
When we pay tribute to our pastor and his wife;
As I unfold this story of their splendor and glory,
Remember, it's all about their life.

Our pastor comes ready to do his job
As a carpenter in every way;
From his bag of tools, he's ready to use,
And he always has something to say.

As he delivers his message each Sunday morning
He's prepared a blueprint for each;
If you follow this guide with the tools he's supplied,
You will learn what he's trying to teach.

He uses examples to deliver his point
He constantly reviews his text;
From Genesis to Revelation, he inspires the congregation,
His manner is never complex.

He opens his "bag" and pulls out his tools
And uses them with confidence and care;
His ultimate goal is to save many souls,
And he's does it with preaching and prayer.

Sister Austin, his wife and faithful companion,
Has a special concern for the youth;
She demands the best with incredible success,
She's nothing but the truth.

While teaching a class or enjoying a show
She puts her whole self in it;
The results are amazing and others are praising
And saying she's truly authentic.

As true believers on a mission for God,
Pastor Austin and his wife are on course,
With their tools at hand and a workable plan,
They perform from a credible source.

As carpenters they work with the tools they possess,
To build on the lives of others;
When their work is complete, from the pulpit to the street,
They've saved many sisters and brothers.

They engage others to complete assigned tasks
From the blueprints provided by them,
They do their part from the very start,
Using vitality, vigor and vim.

Yes, two busy saints, diligently working
And every now and then;
They take the time to relax their minds
And steal away. Amen.

# EBC'S CARPENTERS

When we look at our Lord and Savior Jesus Christ, in his physical life, we see him as a simple carpenter. For those of you who may not know what a carpenter is or does, let me see if I can break it down for you. In man's language, a carpenter builds and repairs houses. He knows the appropriate materials and tools to use. He is skilled in his job. His joy is in the completion and perfection of his works. The Bible doesn't say anything about how skillful Christ was in his physical works, I'm sure that he took pride in what he did in completing his works, but, when we look at the spiritual Christ, we're looking at Christ building and perfecting true or real believers. *1 Corinthians 3:16 "Know ye not that ye are the temple of God, and that the Spirit of God dwelleth in you?"* The spiritual houses that he built during His time were His disciples. Our Lord knows the people who will believe in Him, and so they are the right spiritual materials for the spiritual house.

When I think of Pastor and Sis. Austin, I think of them as spiritual carpenters using their God given skills to build non-believers into true or real believers. As they work to perfect their house, they have had and will continue to have problems along the way. There was a story once where the carpenter's "tools" had a conference. Brother Hammer was in the chair. The meeting had informed him that he must leave because he was too noisy. But he said "If I am to leave this carpenter's shop, brother Gimlet (resembles a corkscrew used to open champagne) must go, too. He is so insignificant that he makes very little impression." Little Brother Gimlet arose and said, "Alright, but Brother Screw must go also. You have to turn him around again and again to get him anywhere." Brother Screw then said, "If you wish, I will go, but Brother Plane must leave also: all his work is on the surface, there is no depth to it." To this Brother Plane replied: "Well, Brother Ruler will have to withdraw if I do, for he is always measuring other folks as though he were the only who is right."
Brother Ruler then complained against Brother Sandpaper, and said,

"I just don't care, he is rougher than he ought to be, and he rubs people the wrong way." In the midst of this discussion, the Carpenter of Nazareth walked in. He had come to perform His day's work. He put on His apron, and went to the bench to build a pulpit. He employed the hammer, the plane, the saw, the gimlet and all the other tools, and used the screw and sandpaper. After the day's work was finished, Brother Saw arose and said, "Brethren, I perceive that all of us are laborers together with God." Likewise, Pastor and Sis. Austin are like the carpenter of Nazareth coming into Emmanuel Baptist Church, bringing together and using the tools to establish a blessed family by employing the talents of many for the benefit of all.

Scripture: 1 Corinthians 12:12, *"For as the body is one, and hath many members, and all the members of that one body, being many, are one body: so also is Christ."*

# INDEX OF TITLES

A.I.D.S. Advising Individuals Devoted to Satan 31

A MISSING SON 83

BEFORE THE FLOOD 75

BEYOND THE OPEN SEA 71

BE A MAN 87

C.I.A. (Christ In Action) 33

CHAINS 25

CHALLENGES 69

CHURCH FOLK: CHURCH MEETING 51

CHURCH FOLK: PASS THE PLATE! 49

CLEAN UP YOUR ACT (Jesus is Coming) 39

D.O.C. 'J' (Depending On Christ) Jesus 35

EBC'S CARPENTERS 135

FATHER TO SON 85

FIRST DATE 91

FLIGHT 27

GOD'S CHOSEN FLOWER
(In memory of Claudia Y. Bullock) 129

HAGAR - by Annel C. Cooke 123

HIJACKED 29

I'LL BE SATISFIED 65

I'LL DO THE BEST I CAN – Rev. P. James Preston, Sr. 5

INTERVENTION 93

IN THE COUNTRY 63

IT NEVER CROSSED MY MIND 67

LABOR OF LOVE 61

LITTLE THINGS 59

MATCHING SHOES (Walking Through Time) 15

| | |
|---|---|
| MESSAGE IN A BOTTLE | 37 |
| MORNING MATTERS | 97 |
| MR. IGGADEE | 103 |
| MY PRAYER | 57 |
| MY SECRET HIDEAWAY | 7 |
| MY WISH | 3 |
| ORDINARY FOLK | 113 |
| RUTH'S RAP - by Annel C. Cooke | 125 |
| SERENITY | 9 |
| SIGNS | 55 |
| THESE TIMES | 77 |
| THE BALLAD OF THE DUMMY - PT 1 | 105 |
| THE BALLAD OF THE DUMMY – PT 2 | 107 |
| THE CANDLE ON THE CORNER | 13 |
| THE CHRISTIAN SOLDIER | 53 |
| THE EMPATHETIC DUMMY | 109 |
| THE ENCOUNTER | 89 |
| THE JADED MASK | 95 |
| THE JAR | 81 |
| THE LIGHTHOUSE | 21 |
| THE PARTY | 45 |
| THE PASSION | 41 |
| THE PROMISE | 79 |
| THE REMORSEFUL THIEF | 43 |
| THE ROADSIDE SHACK | 117 |
| THE ROD | 119 |
| THE SHEPHERD IN THE STICKS | 47 |
| THE SHIP (OF SALVATION) | 11 |
| THE STORM | 115 |
| THE VERSATILE LADY | 101 |

THE WASHING MACHINE                                17

THE WHEELBARROW                                    23

THE WIND                                           19

TRIBUTE TO PASTOR & SIS. AUSTIN– MAY 2004         133

TRIBUTE TO REV. AND SIS. AUSTIN – S.T.A.R.S.      131

# INDEX OF FIRST LINES

| | |
|---|---|
| An Egyptian slave, She stood all alone | 123 |
| A blowing, gentle, whistling breeze | 19 |
| A lost soul faced intolerable odds | 13 |
| A mighty tree was splintered down | 105 |
| A ship is traveling swiftly | 11 |
| Christ is the remedy for all of your problems | 35 |
| Each Sunday as the church doors open | 49 |
| Ever so often, the church will meet | 51 |
| He's off to war in a foreign land | 53 |
| Hey Ruth! | 125 |
| In a lonely woodshed on the outskirts of town | 23 |
| In a southern town, where the cotton grows, | 103 |
| In a town down South in the Carolinas | 101 |
| In life, we move at a steady pace | 59 |
| In our daily lives, we encounter Satan | 25 |
| In the darkness of the hour | 43 |
| In the land of Egypt where the Pharaohs ruled, | 119 |
| In this world of chaos, doubt and confusion | 77 |
| It's time to put away childish things | 87 |
| I make no excuses for the things I've done | 57 |
| I open up my Bible and explore with great concern | 15 |
| I rise up early to start my day | 9 |
| I would have awakened the world today, | 67 |
| Jesus was grabbed and went in peace | 41 |
| Ladies and gents, it's that time again | 133 |
| Lately I've been thinking | 69 |
| Long ago, when I was a child, | 79 |
| My life is filled with ups and downs | 71 |

My wish for you is happiness 3

On a starlit night on the outskirts of town 117

Out of a world of darkness, my mind looks back 27

Sometimes in life we're disillusioned 95

Some man-made signs take control of our lives 55

Some years have passed and the operator is old 109

There's an unusual washing machine 17

There's a lighthouse in the distance 21

There's a message in a bottle pulled from the bay 37

There's a party tonight, bring your invitation 45

There's a rose in a garden of beautiful flowers 129

There are kings, queens and wealthy folk 113

There comes a time in life 31

There is a little country church 47

There is a place I love to go, 7

There is much to do before the flood, 75

The early dawn descending dew 63

The time has come to make decisions 39

Today was the day I planned so long, 91

Trials of life are sure to come, 5

Wake up, my son, and open your eyes 85

Wars and fighting, they take their toll 83

Watch out for Satan, 29

What concerns me most as I rise and shine 97

When I first met you, I was drawn to your beauty, 93

When I see what God has created, 61

When I was young my father left 81

When last we saw Remorseful 107

When the world is rid of Satan and sin 65

When we first met, many years ago, 89

When you stand at the door and extend your hand        33

Years ago, when the world was new,        115

# ABOUT THE AUTHOR –
# Larry W. Colwell

*He was born February 8, 1945, in Columbia Hospital for Women in Washington, DC. He attended Dunbar Senior High, graduating in June of 1962. He furthered his education by attending D.C. Teachers' College from 1962-1967. After receiving his Bachelor of Science degree, he continued his education, earning an M.A.T. Degree (Master of Arts in Teaching) in May 1975, and a Masters Degree in Administration and Supervision in 1982. He has taught in the DC Public Schools for thirty-four years, retiring in June 2000. His inspiration for writing began in 1971. After retirement, he has been concentrating on writing and working with a number of ministries within his church. He is the author of the book: "I'll See You Tomorrow", which is a compilation of inspirational and other types of poems. This book was featured on <u>Heaven 1580AM radio</u> as the book of the month for September, 2005.*

Printed in the United States
60867LVS00004B/1-81

9 781420 892116